A "Noble Bet" in Early Care and Education

Lessons from One Community's Experience

Executive Summary

Brian P. Gill

Jacob W. Dembosky

Jonathan P. Caulkins

Prepared for the
Heinz Endowments

RAND Education

RAND

The research described in this report was supported by the Heinz
Endowments.

ISBN: 0-8330-3198-8

RAND is a nonprofit institution that helps improve policy and
decisionmaking through research and analysis. RAND® is a
registered trademark. RAND's publications do not necessarily reflect
the opinions or policies of its research sponsors.

Published 2002 by RAND
1700 Main Street, P.O. Box 2138, Santa Monica, CA 90407-2138
1200 South Hayes Street, Arlington, VA 22202-5050
201 North Craig Street, Suite 102, Pittsburgh, PA 15213
RAND URL: http://www.rand.org/
To order RAND documents or to obtain additional information,
contact Distribution Services: Telephone: (310) 451-7002;
Fax: (310) 451-6915; Email: order@rand.org

RAND was commissioned by the Heinz Endowments to evaluate the vision, organization, administration, and operation of the Early Childhood Initiative (ECI), a major effort to improve early care and education (ECE) for low-income children from birth through age five in Pittsburgh, Pennsylvania, and the surrounding communities of Allegheny County. ECI was conceived and designed from 1994 to 1996, and operated under the auspices of the United Way (UW) of Allegheny County from 1996 through 2000. Its quality of service and child welfare outcomes are being examined separately by a research team from the University of Pittsburgh and Children's Hospital in Pittsburgh.[1]

RAND's research effort involved, first and foremost, approximately one hundred intensive, confidential interviews with a diverse group of stakeholders: United Way managers, ECI staff, members of the foundation community and other funders, neighborhood representatives, early childhood service providers, business leaders involved in ECI, government officials, academic experts, and early childhood advocates. RAND also obtained and examined a substantial amount of written documentation pertaining to ECI, primarily through the assistance of ECI management and neighborhood agencies. These documents were used not only to understand ECI's history, but also

---

[1]That team's findings to date are reported in S. J. Bagnato, *Quality Early Learning—Key to School Success: A First-Phase Program Evaluation Research Report for Pittsburgh's Early Childhood Initiative (ECI)*, Pittsburgh: Children's Hospital of Pittsburgh, SPECS Evaluation Research Team, 2002.

to examine its enrollment and costs. Finally, the RAND study team explored existing empirical literature on ECE.

Although ECI led to the establishment of new, high-quality ECE services in several communities, it failed to achieve many of its major goals, despite the good intentions of everyone involved and despite the support of a wide array of community leaders. This volume summarizes Brian P. Gill, Jacob W. Dembosky, and Jonathan P. Caulkins, *A "Noble Bet" in Early Care and Education: Lessons from One Community's Experience*, Santa Monica, Calif.: RAND, MR-1544-EDU, 2002, which relays the results of RAND's evaluation.

We sought both to explain why ECI was not more successful and to suggest how future initiatives might produce better results. The report describes ECI's goals and objectives and articulates the breadth of the initiative's ambition to create a comprehensive new system for delivering ECE to low-income children in Allegheny County. It also presents a critical analysis of ECI's business plan and operations, explicating a number of reasons that the initiative fell short of its goals. Finally, since the report aims to be more than a postmortem analysis, it offers lessons for the future, alternative models for ECE initiatives, and public-policy implications. This report should have relevance not only for ECI's stakeholders in Allegheny County, but also for funders, program developers, and policymakers around the country who are working on large-scale initiatives related to a variety of social service reforms.

CONTENTS

FIGURES

ACKNOWLEDGMENTS

This report benefited greatly from assistance from many individuals. First of all, we thank our colleagues Jim Hosek, Becky Kilburn, and Tom Glennan, who advised us on the investigation and analysis at various points. We learned much from their extensive experience and wisdom. Shelley Wiseman helped us improve the organization and writing. Our reviewers, Megan Beckett and Michal Perlman, read the entire draft with care and provided valuable feedback that substantially improved the final report. Jeri O'Donnell and Janet DeLand expertly edited and formatted the report in record time.

We thank Marge Petruska and Maxwell King of the Heinz Endowments for funding the study and giving us the opportunity to carry it out. Mardi Isler deserves special thanks. She was extraordinarily helpful throughout the course of the study in providing a substantial amount of archival material from ECI's records, and she was unfailingly professional in responding to our repeated inquiries. And we thank Charles J. Queenan, Jr., for the phrase "noble bet" that is used in our title.

Our greatest debt is owed to the dozens of individuals who generously gave their time to talk to us about their experiences and insights with respect to the Early Childhood Initiative. These included ECI staff, United Way managers, neighborhood agency representatives, government officials, business leaders, foundation staff, and early childhood service providers. Because we promised respondents that they would remain anonymous, we cannot name them individually here. Without their assistance, however, this study could not have been undertaken.

Chapter One

INTRODUCTION

BACKGROUND AND OBJECTIVES

The Early Childhood Initiative (ECI) of Allegheny County (including the city of Pittsburgh), Pennsylvania, was an ambitious effort to provide high-quality early care and education (ECE) services to at-risk children. Launched in 1996 under the auspices of the United Way (UW) of Allegheny County, ECI aimed within five years to serve 7,600 at-risk children ages zero (birth) to five in 80 low-income neighborhoods, at an average cost of $4,000 to $5,000 per child and a total cost of $59 million over the five-year period. By intervening early in the lives of at-risk children with high-quality services, ECI hoped to improve their preparation for kindergarten, promote their long-term educational attainment, and give them the early tools to help them become productive, successful members of society.

While the long-term benefits of high-quality ECE had been suggested by a number of small-scale, demonstration programs, ECI aimed to be the first in the nation to establish a comprehensive system for delivering high-quality ECE services on a countywide scale. Moreover, ECI intended to provide services through programs that were chosen and operated at the community level by local neighborhood agencies. Finally, ECI aimed to become financially sustainable over the long term, when the initial infusion of dollars from foundations and private donors was exhausted. It planned a lobbying effort to persuade the state of Pennsylvania to commit to fund the initiative at the end of the five-year startup period.

Midway through the fourth year of implementation (2000), when it was clear that the state lobbying effort had failed, that ECI was far

short of its enrollment targets, and that cost per child was significantly higher than expected, ECI planners decided to scale down the
initiative and convert it to a demonstration program. In April 2001,
the program—renamed as the ECI Demonstration Program—was
transferred from UW to the Office of Child Development at the
University of Pittsburgh, where it was placed under new management.

RAND's evaluation, commissioned by the Heinz Endowments (ECI's
largest funder) after ECI had been sharply scaled back, was motivated by the desire to understand why ECI fell short of its objectives
and to learn from its mistakes. The main report—Brian P. Gill, Jacob
W. Dembosky, and Jonathan P. Caulkins, A "Noble Bet" in Early Care
and Education: Lessons from One Community's Experience, Santa
Monica, Calif.: RAND, MR-1544, 2002—summarizes ECI's organizational history, analyzes and explains critical weaknesses that hin-
dered ECI's ability to succeed, and articulates lessons to inform the
design and implementation of future large-scale reform initiatives,
whether in ECE or in other areas of social services. Our findings are
based, first of all, on intensive interviews with nearly one hundred
stakeholders, including UW managers, ECI staff, funders, neighborhood representatives, early childhood service providers, business
leaders involved in ECI, government officials, academic experts, and
early childhood advocates. We also obtained and examined ECI's
documentary records (including business plans, enrollment records,
and financial records), constructed quantitative models to analyze
cost and enrollment data, and explored existing empirical literature
on ECE.

AMBITIOUS AIMS AND MAJOR OBSTACLES

ECI's goals were ambitious. It aimed (1) to provide high-*quality* ECE
services, (2) to do so on a large *scale* (to serve 7,600 children in 80
neighborhoods within five years at a cost of $4,000 to $5,000 per
child), (3) to use a *community*-driven approach, and (4) to achieve
sustainability through a commitment of state funding. Adding
significantly to the challenge were major political, institutional,
economic, and cultural obstacles. These included pervasive low
quality among many of the existing child-care providers, political
ambivalence about the appropriate public role in ECE, possible
underappreciation of the benefits of quality (by policymakers and

parents alike), wide variations in physical and organizational resources in low-income neighborhoods, and the challenges of building a large, new initiative from scratch. One early supporter of ECI in the business community described it publicly as a "noble bet."[1] In our view, that description is quite appropriate. ECI's goals were noble, but their achievement would be difficult and required a calculated gamble. Indeed, to have achieved all of ECI's aims would have been a heroic feat.

The implication is this: *Given the scope of the aims and the scope of the obstacles, success required that ECI have a clear sense of market realities in early care and education, a well-designed theory of action, an effective strategy for inducing a commitment of public funding, and a coherent organizational structure.* This report explains how weaknesses in each of these areas undermined ECI's success in terms of its scale, community, and sustainability goals, if not its quality goals.

IN THIS VOLUME

This executive summary encapsulates the material provided in the main report. Chapter Two examines how well ECI met its goals. Chapter Three addresses structural and organizational issues, and Chapter Four discusses how ECI was transformed by the demands of particular stakeholders. Chapter Five describes the factors that contributed to higher-than-expected costs per child, and Chapter Six examines ECI's effort to achieve long-term sustainability. Finally, Chapter Seven draws lessons from these discussions and offers possible implications for public policy.

---

[1] The term was coined by Charles J. Queenan, Jr., a prominent Pittsburgh attorney.

Chapter Two

THE BOTTOM LINE

Although evidence from a separate evaluation suggests that ECI may have succeeded in promoting high-quality ECE programs, it was far less successful in achieving its other goals.

QUALITY

Quality of service and child welfare outcomes, which were not part of RAND's charge, are being examined separately by the SPECS (Scaling Progress in Early Childhood Settings) team from the University of Pittsburgh and Children's Hospital in Pittsburgh. RAND did not review the SPECS methods, so we simply note the findings to date of the SPECS team here. According to the SPECS report,[1] ECI succeeded in promoting quality in participating ECE programs and favorable outcomes for participating children. More specifically, the report states that ECI children demonstrated effective social and behavioral skills and that they went on to succeed in kindergarten and first grade, as measured by low rates of grade retention and referral to special education. The findings reported by the SPECS team are substantially what ECI's planners aimed to achieve for participating children.

---

[1] S. J. Bagnato, *Quality Early Learning—Key to School Success: A First-Phase Program Evaluation Research Report for Pittsburgh's Early Childhood Initiative (ECI)*, Pittsburgh: Children's Hospital of Pittsburgh, SPECS Evaluation Research Team, 2002.

SCALE

At its peak (around May 2000), ECI served only about 680 children, which is one-quarter of the number expected to be served at that point in time and less than one-tenth of the total number targeted for service.

While ECI served fewer children than intended, its hours of service per child were higher than intended because, contrary to the plan's assumption that most children would be in part-day services, virtually all children were in full-day services. Even accounting for this difference, however, ECI at its peak was providing only about half as many child-hours of service as the original business plan had intended for that point in time.

Even if ECI had been able to scale up more quickly, it could not have served 7,600 children, because costs per child were substantially higher than expected. In 1999 (year three of implementation), ECI's cost averaged $13,612 per child-year.[2] Although this is not dramatically different from the cost of some other, widely cited high-quality ECE interventions,[3] it is three times as high as the cost expected in the original business plan ($4,407 in year three). As we discuss in depth throughout this report, the business plan made a number of mistakes that contributed to the underestimation of costs. Here we mention three reasons that were prominent. First, ECI provided far more hours of service per child than the plan anticipated, because virtually all children were served in full-day programs. Second, the plan assumed that operational cost per child was the same at all levels of enrollment, failing to recognize that cost per child is inevitably substantially higher for providers that are less than 100 percent enrolled. Third, ECI's plan required a substantial bureaucratic

---

[2]1999 was the last full year of ECI's full-scale operation (as well as the last year for which we were able to obtain financial data). Details on the methodology and assumptions for calculating costs are provided in the Appendix to the main report, (Gill et al., 2002).

[3]For example, the High/Scope Perry Preschool Project cost an estimated $12,148 per child (in 1996 dollars). See Lynn A. Karoly, Peter W. Greenwood, Susan S. Everingham, Jill Houbé, M. Rebecca Kilburn, C. Peter Rydell, Matthew Sanders, and James R. Chiesa, *Investing in Our Children: What We Know and Don't Know About the Costs and Benefits of Early Childhood Interventions*, Santa Monica, Calif.: RAND, MR-898, 1998.

structure both centrally and at the neighborhood level, and it was unduly optimistic about the administrative costs associated with this structure.

COMMUNITY

ECI's community-driven approach had some successes and a number of failures. Devolution of authority to the neighborhood level succeeded in a few neighborhoods where local leaders eagerly joined the ECI process and established plans that led to a strong working relationship with ECI management (ECIM) and, ultimately, the creation of new, high-quality ECE programs operated by neighborhood-based agencies. Moreover, community leaders in a number of neighborhoods affected by ECI joined together to establish an ongoing support and advocacy network for early childhood and school readiness issues.

But disappointment is widespread in many of the neighborhoods that were targeted by ECI. Some local leaders felt that ECI did not live up to its promise of permitting neighborhoods to define their needs and the ECE services they wanted. In their view, ECI's process for approving neighborhood plans imposed unreasonable delays, and ECI imposed a narrow definition of quality that precluded local discretion. This left substantial resentment in some neighborhoods, especially those that did not get an early start in the process and were eventually cut off when ECI was scaled down in 2000. Even in neighborhoods that successfully launched ECE programs under ECI's sponsorship, lead agencies felt undermined by constantly changing program rules and requirements.

SUSTAINABILITY

Although ECI helped to raise the profile of ECE as an important policy issue in communities around Pennsylvania and in state government, it failed in its explicit goal of achieving a state commitment to support the initiative with public funds. An effort to change the initiative to make better use of existing state funding streams was only partly successful, and it led to a power struggle over the direction of ECI, as well as to frustration and resentment in the neighborhoods. The sustainability of the two remaining neighborhood agencies supported by ECI has not yet been demonstrated and will be a major goal for these agencies over the next three years while their foundation funding continues.

POSITIVE ASPECTS OF ECI'S LEGACY

ECI's failure to achieve its greatest ambitions should not obscure the positive aspects of its legacy. ECI helped to build the capacity of a number of low-income neighborhoods to provide ECE services that are apparently of high quality. It succeeded in helping several Head Start providers become licensed to provide full-day services. It increased public awareness of the importance of quality in Pittsburgh and around the state and reportedly motivated quality improvements in some major nonparticipating child-care centers in Allegheny County. And it demonstrated the ability of the Pittsburgh community to mobilize large-scale support and funding from diverse constituencies and people with differing political perspectives. Finally, ECI's troubles serve to illuminate the serious public-policy dilemmas associated with ECE.

We now turn to the major task of the report: explaining the mistakes that undermined ECI's success with respect to its scale, community, and sustainability goals.

Chapter Three

STRUCTURAL CHALLENGES

At the time of ECI's inception, no models existed of high-quality ECE delivered on a large scale through grassroots, neighborhood control. ECI therefore needed to develop its own "theory of action" to explain how the initiative would work. According to the theory of action developed by the original planners (depicted in Figure 3.1), ECI was to have a central administration (housed within UW) that would fund, supervise, and monitor (with stringent quality standards) lead agencies in each community. Each lead agency would in turn fund and supervise the participating ECE providers, which would serve children and their families. In addition, the central administration (ECI management, or ECIM) was to provide technical assistance to lead agencies, which would in turn provide such assistance to ECE providers.

This theory of action proved to be cumbersome and problematic. While most of ECI's theory of action concerned the central administration and neighborhood agencies, the ultimate goals of high-quality ECE services for large numbers of children around the county were to be served by the relationship between providers and families. ECI's theory of action created an extensive structure above that relationship rather than addressing it more directly. This put several layers of organization between the funders and the primary intended beneficiaries (i.e., the children to be served) and led to a number of implementation problems.

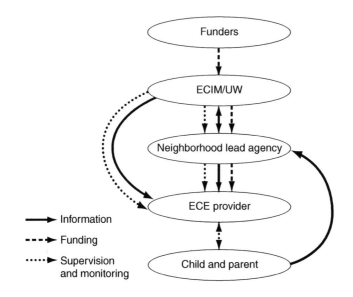

Figure 3.1—ECI's Theory of Action

ADMINISTRATIVE COSTS

One consequence of ECI's multilayered theory of action was that each layer of administration added to the initiative's cost. The original business plan projected that the cost of ECI's central administration at UW would amount to $286 per child (or 6.5 percent of a total cost of $4,407 per child) in year three of implementation. In fact, central administrative costs in year three (1999) were $1,231 per child (or 9 percent of the total cost of $13,612). The theory of action simultaneously imposed substantial top-down requirements and created additional structures in each neighborhood, making high administrative costs inevitable.

THE CHALLENGES OF COMMUNITY CONTROL

At the same time it established a hierarchical bureaucracy, ECI's theory of action aimed to permit neighborhoods to direct participating local programs. Devolution of authority to the community level requires a tradeoff: Neighborhood-led programs may be more robust and effective than those imposed from the outside, but implementation is not likely to proceed quickly. ECI's planners failed to appreciate how much time neighborhood groups would need to mobilize, assess residents' needs, identify space for child-care centers, develop detailed proposals, and establish programs.

ECI's business plan did not acknowledge the extent to which quality control and community control might be in tension. ECI's insistence on its own definition of quality inevitably placed constraints on the degree of freedom to be exercised by communities. When ECI was launched, neighborhoods were told to "dream big"; some were disappointed when they found that their dreams were not always consistent with the vision of ECIM. Although neighborhood agencies endorsed the principle of high-quality service provision, some chafed under a quality monitoring process that they perceived as excessively rigid.

A FLAWED ADMINISTRATIVE STRUCTURE

Compounding these problems was a complicated administrative structure for ECI's leadership. ECI lacked an independent board with the authority to resolve conflicts and make key decisions. ECIM staff were nominally UW employees, but they were never comfortably integrated into the larger UW organization. ECIM reported to several different UW managers at different points in time, often lacking a clear chain of command. A proliferation of volunteer oversight committees further confused administration and diffused authority. And when key staff departed, individuals who had been hired to serve a specific role were given responsibilities outside their primary experience and expertise.

ECI's complex leadership structure had several negative consequences. First, the community planning process was slow, because plans had to be reviewed by several layers of committees. Second, the response to changing conditions related to the increased demand for full-day services was slow. Third, confusion over who had the authority to make key operational and strategic decisions permitted disagreements between ECIM and UW management to escalate into full-blown, unresolved power struggles.

ECIM and UW management prioritized the goals of the initiative differently. For ECIM, maintaining high quality was the paramount goal. UW management worried about serving substantial numbers of children and achieving sustainability. When costs per child turned out to be much higher than expected, ECI's goals came into tension with each other, putting ECIM and UW management at loggerheads. The weakness of the organizational structure delayed the conflict's resolution. Communication with funders and business leaders broke down because UW management and ECIM disagreed over what they should be telling these stakeholders. At the community level, lead agencies and providers received mixed signals about ECI rules and procedures. As a result, support for ECI declined among funders and business leaders, and confidence in the initiative suffered in the neighborhoods.

Chapter Four

SUPPLY, DEMAND, AND INCENTIVES

ECI's original business plan made assumptions about the population of children that would be served, the mix of services (e.g., full-day versus half-day, center versus family child-care) that would be provided, and the participation of existing ECE providers. Many of these assumptions turned out to be far off the mark, largely because the planners paid insufficient attention to demand, supply, and incentives. A number of ECI's problems that were related to enrollment and costs might have been avoided if the business plan had better anticipated how parents, ECE providers, and neighborhood agencies would respond to ECI.

THE DEMAND FOR FULL-DAY, CENTER-BASED SERVICES

The business plan failed to anticipate that parents and neighborhood agencies might gravitate toward the highest-cost option among the services ECI offered, which ranged from part-day, Head Start–like enrichment and literacy programs to full-day, center-based care and education. The plan assumed that 71 percent of children would be served in low-cost, part-day programs. In fact, virtually all children were served in full-day programs, most in new centers. Hence, one major reason that ECI cost more per child than expected was that ECI provided more intensive services (on average) than expected.

ECI underestimated the demand for full-time programs in part because it underestimated the proportion of eligible children whose mothers were in the workforce. Welfare reform—passed in Pennsylvania in the summer of 1996—was relevant in bringing women into the workforce, but low-income mothers had already been joining the labor force in growing numbers prior to welfare reform. Moreover, a parental preference for full-day care is unsurprising if parents are given a choice of full- or part-day care and both options are largely or entirely subsidized. Large numbers of parents—whether low- or high-income, employed or not—are likely to prefer more hours of child care and education if they are offered at little or no additional cost. This is essentially the choice that ECI offered. The incentives for neighborhood agencies were similar: Told by ECI to "dream big," most sought to establish new child-care centers.

THE COST OF RELYING ON NEW PROVIDERS

Although the business plan expected that many existing providers would be used, in practice many were left out. This occurred for three reasons. First, ECIM believed that many existing providers operated at so low a level of quality that they were incapable of providing high-quality services. Second, some community planning groups chose to exclude existing providers. Third, some existing providers chose not to participate, either because they considered the quality standards and monitoring process too intrusive or because they were informal, unregistered providers not wishing to become part of the formal child-care system. ECI's greater-than-expected reliance on new providers meant that it could not reach as many children as hoped and resulted in higher capital costs as well.

Extensive reliance on new centers also meant that ECI had to endure the high costs of the startup period, during which center staff have to be employed but enrollment is relatively low. More generally, ECI's original business plan mistakenly assumed that centers that were less than fully enrolled could serve children for the same cost per child as fully enrolled centers could (i.e., it assumed that operating costs at a center were fully variable). Such an assumption might have been reasonable for pre-existing centers, for which ECI intended to provide a capitated reimbursement amount for each child served. In fact, however, the great majority of ECI children were served in newly established centers. Line item funding was provided for new centers, which needed to hire staff prior to enrolling their first children. This meant that in practice the centers' operating costs were largely fixed, regardless of the number of children served.

When ECI centers opened, enrollments grew gradually over time and in most cases never reached 100 percent of capacity. In 1999, average enrollment in ECI centers was 72.6 percent of capacity (increasing over the course of the year). As a result, operating cost per child was higher than projected in the original business plan. The fault here lies not with the lead agencies or the providers, but with the variable-cost assumption of the original business plan, which was not realistic.

Chapter Five

EXPLAINING ECI'S COSTS

The total cost per child in 1999 ($13,612) was 3.1 times as high as the expected cost ($4,407). The planners underestimated all components of cost: operating, capital, and administrative. Using simulations to correct some of the mistaken assumptions of the original business plan, we were able to estimate the magnitude of different drivers of ECI's cost overruns. Figure 5.1 depicts ECI's original cost projections, its actual costs, and the results of two simulations.

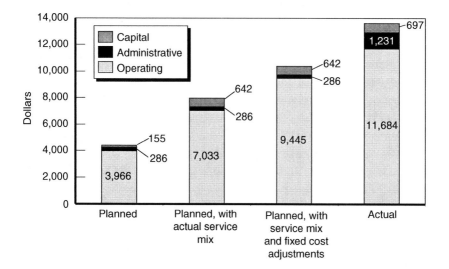

Figure 5.1—Effect of Service Mix and Fixed Costs on Cost per Child-Year, 1999

The second bar in the figure shows the results of adjusting the original cost projections using the actual service mix provided by ECI in 1999. The shift to full-day, center-based services dramatically increased both operating and capital costs. If the business plan had anticipated the actual service mix, its estimate of the expected cost per child would have risen from $4,407 to $7,961.

The third bar accounts not only for the actual service mix, but also for the fixed costs of operating new child-care centers. The simulation in this case was based on incomplete data, so the results should be interpreted cautiously. Because a portion of operating costs may be variable, the estimate represents an upper bound. Nevertheless, it makes clear that the ECI business plan substantially underestimated costs because it did not recognize that operating costs in new centers would be largely fixed. If the business plan had accounted for fixed costs and anticipated the actual service mix, its estimate of the expected cost per child would have risen to as much as $10,373.

In total, the two flawed assumptions explain as much as 65 percent of the difference between the planned and actual cost per child (again, this is an upper-bound estimate). Figure 5.2 shows how central administrative costs and additional operating and capital costs

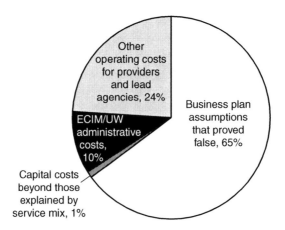

Figure 5.2—Factors Explaining the Difference Between Planned and Actual Cost per Child-Year, 1999

(not already explained by the service mix) compare to the flawed business plan assumptions in explaining the total difference between planned and expected cost per child. Higher-than-expected central administrative costs account for 10 percent of the difference. Capital costs beyond those attributable to the service mix explain less than 1 percent of the difference. After accounting for underestimates related to service mix, fixed operating costs, capital costs, and central administrative costs of ECIM and UW, the remaining neighborhood-level costs for lead agencies and service provision explain 24 percent of the difference between expected and actual cost per child (which may be a slight underestimate if the fixed cost adjustment is overestimated).

The interpretation of ECI's total cost of $13,612 per child depends to a great extent on the frame of reference. Compared to the budgeted amount of $4,407, it seems astonishingly high. But it is important to remember that high-quality, full-day ECE programs generally cost substantially more than $4,407. Nevertheless, it is clear that ECI's business plan and operation ensured that costs would be dramatically higher than expected. The theory of action virtually guaranteed that administrative costs would be high. In addition, planners failed to anticipate the predictable demands of parents and lead agencies, which moved the initiative toward providing the more-expensive, full-time, center-based care. Indeed, ECI ultimately looked quite different from what many of its original advocates and funders had intended.

Chapter Six

THE EFFORT TO SECURE STATE SUPPORT

ECI's plan to secure state funding ultimately failed because of existing obstacles and the particular strategy pursued. The obstacles were many. First, the benefits of high-quality ECE programs are diffuse, whereas the costs are concentrated. A strong societal benefit/cost ratio may not be sufficient to persuade the state to foot the bill when many of the benefits will not accrue to the state's treasury. Second, most of the benefits of high-quality ECE programs accrue over the long term (e.g., program participants not getting involved in crime as teenagers and adults), whereas the costs are borne up front. Third, the amount of funding that planners hoped the state would contribute to ECI—most of the $26 million annual cost when it reached countywide scale—was large enough that it would inevitably raise issues of regional fairness among Pennsylvania political leaders.

Finally, voters and policymakers were and still are ambivalent about public funding of ECE. Some voters and policymakers feel strongly that child care is a private responsibility of parents rather than a public responsibility of the state. The views of leadership at the state level clearly make a difference, and, despite growing support for public funding of ECE in many states, Pennsylvania's state government has a history of conservatism when it comes to funding ECE programs.

Independent of these obstacles, ECI's strategy for obtaining state funding was misguided. First, although ECI planners made some attempts to engage state officials, they did not ensure that state policymakers had a full, substantive, and early role in the initiative's design.

Second, and more fundamentally, ECI came into conflict with the goals and operation of Pennsylvania's existing system of child-care subsidies for low-income families. The shift in the ECI service mix to full-day programs switched its public identification from an education initiative to a child-care initiative and increased its financial dependence on the existing state system of child-care subsidies. ECI's initial conflict with the state subsidy system stemmed from its failure to acknowledge the state's preference for parental choice in child care. ECI also came into conflict with the state's desire, via welfare reform, to induce parents on public assistance to enter the workforce. ECI's primary goal was to provide high-quality early education to low-income children—regardless of whether their parents were working. The primary goal of the state child-care subsidy system, by contrast, is to provide incentives and means for parents receiving public assistance to move into the workforce. Even if ECI's planners disagreed with the state's priorities, it was important to recognize that a direct conflict with those priorities would seriously undermine the likelihood of state support for ECI.

This conflict became a serious operational problem for ECI as it became increasingly dependent on the state's existing subsidy system. UW sought to reduce costs and make ECI more compatible with the state subsidy system, but its efforts created major internal conflicts and undermined ECI's support in the neighborhoods. Moreover, these efforts did not ultimately reduce costs enough to make ECI sustainable using existing or foreseeable levels of state subsidies.

Chapter Seven

CONCLUSIONS

LESSONS FOR THE FUTURE

ECI's weaknesses suggest a number of lessons for future large-scale reform initiatives:

- Planners should focus on clear goals and well-defined services. In ECI's case, its quality, scale, and community-control goals often came into conflict with each other, especially when different stakeholders prioritized the goals differently or defined quality differently.

- An ambitious, large-scale initiative should have an independent board and a clear administrative structure that promotes strong leadership.

- A clean, direct theory of action more effectively promotes an initiative's goals.

- Careful consideration of demand, supply, and responses to incentives is essential to anticipating unintended consequences.

- Planners should make every effort to include all relevant stakeholders early in the planning process.

- Critical, independent review is essential from the start. Review should be conducted by someone who can identify flaws without fear of retribution, is not a member of the original advocacy group, has appropriate substantive expertise, and will invest time and energy in the review commensurate with the project's importance.

- Large-scale initiatives benefit from a substantial investment in planning and often are well served by initial piloting on a smaller scale.

- Bold visions require hardheaded plans that acknowledge political and policy realities.

ALTERNATIVE MODELS FOR ECE REFORM

We gathered information on four promising ECE initiatives currently operating in Pennsylvania and elsewhere. The Chicago Child-Parent Center program operates through the Chicago public schools, offering high-quality preschool to low-income children. In southeastern Pennsylvania, Child Care Matters is a UW-operated initiative that works to improve the quality of existing ECE providers by providing them with technical assistance and resources as well as a "quality supplement" incentive if they become accredited with the National Association for the Education of Young Children (NAEYC). Focus on Our Future, in York, Pennsylvania, likewise provides resources to promote accreditation; it also funds professional development for ECE workers. In Chicago, Focus on Quality has helped over 100 centers become accredited with NAEYC, while a public awareness campaign has promoted parental awareness of the value of high-quality ECE. Formal evaluation results are as yet available for only one of these programs (the Chicago Child-Parent Centers), but we believe that each program represents a promising approach that funders, policymakers, and ECE practitioners may wish to consider. These programs by no means constitute the full array of promising ECE initiatives. Nevertheless, each suggests an alternative approach to scaling up high-quality ECE services. In contrast to ECI, each has a narrower focus on a more limited number of goals. None places much emphasis on the goal of community control, and most focus on existing providers, thereby making the scale-up process more straightforward and usually faster.

Future large-scale ECE initiatives might consider any of these possibilities, or might instead consider a parent-centered approach. For example, planners might choose to distribute funds as quality-focused supplements to the existing state subsidy system. Parents would be permitted to use "quality vouchers" at any provider that met a designated quality standard. If an existing standard, such as

NAEYC accreditation, is considered insufficient, a separate quality monitoring system could be established to identify high-quality providers and enforce standards. Additional grants might be available to providers seeking to improve their quality in order to become eligible for the "quality vouchers."

We do not mean to suggest that pursuing a community-driven approach is necessarily bad. But funders, program planners, and policymakers need to understand that community-driven processes inevitably take time. Moreover, communities may have desires and interests that differ from those of the planners; in consequence, an approach that takes the community's desires seriously must be prepared to accept results that may differ from those the planners and funders originally intended. An approach that simultaneously aims to permit community control and to impose top-down bureaucratic control may well lead to disappointment on all sides.

Although we found no examples among the initiatives described above, there may be models that would both take the community's desires more seriously and provide more appropriate incentives, permitting communities to "dream big" while controlling costs and ensuring quality. In addition, it is worth pointing out that parent-centered models are implicitly community based because they are driven by the desires of parents in the community.

IMPLICATIONS FOR PUBLIC POLICY

As ECI's planners recognized, inducing large and sustained changes in the ECE universe requires public action. State and federal policymakers can exercise substantial influence over conditions in the ECE market, if they choose to do so. The ECI experience raises several broad public-policy issues that may provide guidance for policymakers.

The first such issue concerns the demand for quality. Evidence suggests that parents do not have a high demand for high-quality ECE services, at least as understood by ECE experts.[1] But parental knowl-

---

[1] David M. Blau, *The Child Care Problem: An Economic Analysis*, New York: Russell Sage, 2001.

edge and preferences are not set in stone. Policymakers (and local planners) may be able to increase the demand for high-quality services through public awareness campaigns and parent education efforts.

Policymakers may also wish to directly address quality in child care. One increasingly popular approach to raising the quality of ECE services is a tiered subsidy system. Under such a system, each provider receives a per-child subsidy based on the provider's level of quality. Providers then have an incentive to improve their quality. States have the discretion to use federal welfare funds to raise subsidy amounts for higher-quality providers; many have already done so. In addition, greater public investment in the education and training of ECE workers might serve as a useful complement to a tiered subsidy system.

ECI illuminates the tension that exists between two purposes: serving needy children and providing incentives for parents to work. In most states (including Pennsylvania), the primary purpose of child-care subsidy systems for low-income parents is to encourage them to move off welfare and into the labor force. A substantial number of low-income children are ineligible for subsidies because their parents do not meet the requirements of welfare-reform laws. In consequence, any ECE policy that is tied to welfare laws will fail to reach many at-risk children. Policymakers who wish to promote the availability of high-quality ECE services for all disadvantaged children need to take a different approach.

Many policymakers and voters resist the idea of separating child-care subsidies from employment requirements. They often see employment requirements not only as a way to provide appropriate incentives to welfare mothers, but also as a way to distinguish between "deserving" and "undeserving" poor in the distribution of government benefits. Whether this latter purpose is appropriate is a matter of basic values, such as fairness and justice, and is not easily susceptible to empirical policy analysis. But policymakers may wish to consider the costs to society of a child-care policy that focuses on the deservingness of parents rather than the welfare of children.